It No Longer Rains Like Before

It No Longer Rains Like Before

Ibohal Kshetrimayum

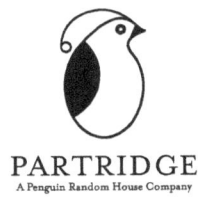

PARTRIDGE

A Penguin Random House Company

To order additional copies of this book, contact
Partridge India
000 800 10062 62
orders.india@partridgepublishing.com

www.partridgepublishing.com/india

To my mother, in whose lullaby I heard dreams.

Foreword

Ibohal Kshetrimayum's poems do not lend themselves to the stereotypical clichés often deployed by the regular critics and anthologists in their discussions of the poetry of north-east India. In fact, the stereotype is an illusion as much as the North-east itself, which is an amorphous, vaguely defined construct of the mainstream imagination. North-east India, as anyone who has been there or has even looked closely at its culture and literature will testify, is itself as diverse as India with its many languages, cultures and subcultures, belief systems, forms of worship, oral traditions, and genres of written literature. Just as we need a comparative paradigm and not a composite one to understand the literatures of India, we will need a critical strategy that looks both at the shared and the specific aspects of the literature of the North-east—which is no more than a convenient umbrella term more geopolitical than aesthetic—to discuss its literary corpus.

Ibohal is a poet of images; his poetry has an unfailing visual impact. Look at the very opening poem, for example, which has these imagery: the blind laughing in the heart, the woman's hair darkening the dream's path, the sea roaring in her curls, an animal felt on her skin, a burning river rushing out of her crevice, a cuckoo crying for the moon's silver drops, the dawn coming with a yawn, the coconut trees bending to comb her dishevelled clouds, the heart lost in the crumpled pillows, drinking mountains from a bottle of sunsets, the moon moaning for a window. Concrete and semi-abstract images, accompanied by colours and sounds as in a multimedia manifestation, strikingly capture the feelings of love, desire, and desolation in the poet's heart. At times the images can be strikingly exotic, like 'your ebony breasts flapped like a pair of vanilla pods from Madagascar, slapping me with the sandy flames of Sahara' ('Perfumes'), or semi-abstract as in 'the western horizon cremating the past where we could have been' ('Wet Curls'). At times they are images of metamorphosis. 'The drunken fathers become sad winds. / Engulfed by the chaotic madness, they lost their daughters' ('Bardoishikhla'). At other times, they are magical. 'Needles of rain fell on a puddle, became infant circles / which died after three tiny ripples, and my heart skipped / a beat for the bubble we broke that night, / which was almost a placenta' ('Fear') or 'In the hills of seven huts, / where *war* is either a place or surname, / and dreams are translated into numbers, / and a number became a gambler's sad song, / I found God breathing through the pine trees' ('In the Hills of Seven Huts').

In a casual conversation we had while travelling together from Shillong to Nartiang, Ibohal told me how he can only wait for poems to come to him—and never force a poem out of himself. And they often come in the form of scenes and images, often in his dreams, which he just writes down and organizes tightly in the terse structure of a poem. That may be the secret of the dreamy, dusky, revelatory quality of these poems that seem to emerge from that twilight zone of the subconscious mind with the force of magic and ritual.

There are times too when they acquire the quality of legends. 'Black' (the meaning of the name of the poet's friend Musuk in Manipuri) is an example. It is the real tale of a childhood friend who died in 1974, but in the poem, it takes on the colours of a legend, with a bit of drama thrown in. Black was a thief; people hated him. Only the poet knew his 'other colours'. He loved the same girl as the poet did and won her over, wearing a shirt stolen from the poet so that he would look clean—which he returned to the poet later with an apology. And one cold morning in January, his body was found hanging from a tree. The jealous were happy, but his beloved's tears said he had actually been murdered. The poet has now forgiven him for his love for the girl and the stolen shirt, and he keeps the shirt clean in his painful memory. The shirt has grown into a symbol that connects all the three characters central to the whole narrative.

'Shipih's Journey' is another narrative of the kind. Shipih, a half Khasi born to an outsider, is introduced in the very opening lines. 'Forty-seven years old, / but he remains lost at eleven. / He smiles at dogs and people / with effortless honesty.' He walks rolling an iron ring all the time and talks to that wheel. One day he tells the wheel that they will follow the sun till they find the east and then trails westwards 'under a coughing sky'.

Durga is another character that gives her name to a poem. She was the village whore who warmed the speaker's nights and would always tell him she wanted to be a goddess. Then she became mad, and once out of the madhouse, she began to roam the streets, singing strange songs. One day she stole a sari from a sinking idol on the day of immersion and wore it herself. She was pursued by the pious and was stoned. The poet saw her forehead bleeding but walked away like a coward. 'I looked back at an idol and remembered: / the goddess was actually born in a mound on the courtyard of a whore!'

Or look at the poem on Thynroit, a Khasi village. The poet looks at the village with amused detachment. 'A middle-aged village drunk / shouts obscene warnings to a black bull / for molesting his wife's cow grazing nearby. / The village masseur sits on a rickety chair / and waits for city clients with broken limbs. / Screaming urchins in dirty red, blue, and pink gumboots / stampede on the dusty path to the crowded watershed / where their aunts and sisters wash smudged linens.' But suddenly the poem takes an eerie turn when the night transforms the village and urges him to recall a village he had once left behind. 'But when the sun sets behind the emptying hills / after the church doors have been locked / and the good book has been closed for the day, / a calm silence settles down on the village, / and the moon takes the shape of a clipped fingernail / while a dog barks at it in wolfish superstition. / Between echoes of mothers calling their children home, / Thynroit urges me to remember a village / in a faraway land I left behind.'

And there is Lazarus of Bollongre. A truck rams him from behind while he is peeing on the fence of the Nehru Park, and he is no Lazarus of the Holy Book to be called back to life ('Lazarus's Onward Journey').

This search for the lost roots and the lost people of the past is followed up further in another poem 'A Cruise to the Past', where the poet is in search of his folks lost during the devastating Burmese attack on his land in 1819. It begins by alluding to his obsession with the past. 'Friends of the family say / that I inherited this obstinate habit / of chasing mice in my head / from my promiscuously adventurous grandpa, / who could live with ease in the cramped and babbling company / of my four grandmas under one roof!'

He knows it is like searching for a needle in a haystack, but he has inherited a 'genetic agitation' from his grandfather that sends him on a cruise down the river Chindwin to where it meets Irrawaddy. Following the 'footprint of an unknown smile', he reaches a red-light street and finds himself in a nightclub with a girl, a schoolteacher who had fallen on bad days, offering her body for 1,000 kyat. He gives her the money but rejects the offer. The search then takes him to a Meitei Brahmin family where the father offers his daughter to him in marriage, hoping he would take her back to Manipur, where they belonged. The daughter too joins her father in the request, but again, the poet excuses himself and goes up a hill to meet the monk at the pagoda who only expresses his anger when the poet mentions the name of General Than Shwe, whom he thought would help him as this general is abusive even of Aung Suu Kyi. His search leads him nowhere, and he is left with the feeling that he shares with that Brahmin girl. 'I am as rootless as you are.'

The pain of loss is also reflected in the poem 'I Won't Walk on It', where the poet speaks of 'our ancestral acres now reduced to a mossy courtyard'. If his toddler niece refuses to walk on the untilled land, he himself refuses to walk on the road 'amidst randomly pointed rifles'. The same sense of loss characterizes the poem 'Rain Dance'. 'My mother puts on her royal attire / to do the rain dance of a princess, / but her feet are barren, / for it no longer rains like before.'

Ibohal is no less political than most of his contemporaries, like Yumlembam Ibomcha Singh and Thangjam Ibopishak, but he carries his politics lightly and gracefully. His aggressiveness seldom shows as in 'For Some Reasons', where he mourns the destiny of his land, whose history he doubts for its existence in a country that questions his citizenship and identifies its inclusiveness within an exclusive culture. 'I drag a corpse / whose funeral / is kept at abeyance / until you see my face.' The poet powerfully sums up the fate of his people in this single image in 'Invisible Man'.

In another poem, 'Misfortune', he again speaks of his identity that renders him alien in his country. 'My face, language, and colour say I'm a misfit / To live in your country or even be called your brother.' Even his father thought he was misbegotten. 'If you really want to know me, come closer behind me, and I will / Break the mirror with a stone—and there you'll see me in my worthlessness. / And you'll understand the mishap of broken faces.'

Even when he thinks of his debts and obligations, overwhelmed by a sense of guilt and thinks of crucifying himself, he is looking for a 'deep-rooted tree' ('Debts').

At times the homesickness gets projected on to the natural world as when, in the 'History of Our Rice', he mourns the loss of the old rice fields that had varieties of rice with specific aromas. The poem ends ironically, suggesting the contemporary state of things in Manipur. 'Rife with hostility, / roots dare not grow in caking mud, and / we no longer see startled catfish / and lazy earthworms when we walk / through young rice fields. / Perhaps we should plant guns in our fields, / and hopefully bullets will become rice and / we'll die without bleeding, a nobler way/ to end the history.'

'Is This My Home?' also reflects this feeling of loss. 'Memories only live here. / But even the shadows of my childhood / had been moved.' He feels everyone at home is only playing an assigned role. 'I as a good lover and a son. / You as a jubilant bird who has found a new cage. / My father as a man who at last could show off his nothingness / when he justifies the statute disqualifying mother / from sitting alongside him on the same mat in public. / Your friend as a Good Samaritan, silently enjoying the irony. / My mother smiling joyfully on her final satire / when she lights the cigarette I bought for her in public. / And the act completes with the ultimate dance / of a shrew's broom sweeping away my footprints / from the ruins of my grandfather's dreams / while my brother remains possessed by her spells.'

Elsewhere he complains: 'I am not even a dream, / Which could follow a crow's flight' ('I Am Not Even a Dream'). The poet is very clear about the mission of poetry, reminding us of Ceslaw Milosz's warning: 'The poet remembers.' 'You can kill the poet but not the poem, / For what is written remains written . . . Even if you could kill the poet, remember, don't let his / Blood spill, for it will turn into ink, and you'll be drowned. / And even you, a colonial offshoot, will mouth poetry, / Infected by his madness, even as your lungs suffocate / With that vision of indignant displeasure waiting for you / On the sea's bed salted with blood from my brothers.'

There are also moments of tender love, separation, and reunion in Ibohal's poetry. Look at the poem 'And the Train Leaves without Her'. His beloved leaves him, and he is haunted by her memory. The community accuses him of being an irresponsible drunkard who has ruined her. 'Daybreak brought injurious winds, which mocked me / with such fierce jibes: "Your invincible groin's pride had caused / a lily to shed its dimples, and look at you—a malicious drunk." / I knew no star will be named after me, / but I swore to stain the sky with my blood and / discourage conspirators from transforming our love / into a weighty theme of city gossip / before a choppy sea of rumours drowns all dreams.' But one day she comes back with a baby whose eyes are searching for an answer, never to leave again.

The same tenderness marks the poem 'Anxiety'. 'How I wish every day to wade / In the swamp of your hairs / Cut a reed and blow a precipitous tune / To awake the dots of your sleeping rabbits / Or surrender myself to a blackbird's beak / Pecking at a cloud for milk / While you spread your tresses / Sprawling on the snow of your dreams / Making my existence spurious / In this place where winds whisper poetry / To moist pine needles / Multiplying my anxiety of your absence / In my journey through deserts of wrinkled sheets.'

In 'Wet Curls', he wonders: 'What shall I do in heaven now / without your moist locks? . . . What shall I do with blossoms / if I can't fasten them to your hair?'

In 'Autumn's Sweet Hurting', he says: 'First day of autumn, / far more sacred almost / than my own birthday. / For on this day, / a long time ago, I fell in love with / a breeze falling from your tresses.'

'The Second Best' opens like this: 'My love was naked, and she didn't hide. / My heart flew away chasing a raven, her clothes, and / my body covered her nakedness. / When she moved, everything moved—our bodies, / earth, and blood.'

Ibohal easily invokes the atmosphere of his land with references to the landscape, names of trees and plants, customs and rituals, myths, legends and archetypes, ways of life and kinship, sights, sounds, and smells. He has a whole poem inspired by smells titled 'Smells'. 'I smelt milk in my room, / when she entered wearing a cloud / borrowed from the sky-blue curtain. / Her breasts were wet with milk, / eager to wean an infant poem, / but I wasn't ready to grow. / She then melted, / her milk with the smell of / a wet crow flying off with a broken wing / from the sunset ripples of the river, her lover! / In my hills, breasts and udders have roots, / and milk smells like earth.'

Let me end these ruminations quoting the short poem 'A Land of Ripples', which sums up the poet's anger, despair, and frustration:

A land where guns are no longer fired in anger
but in deceitful dreams.
A land where people starve for a peaceful recipe
till they are no longer hungry.
A land where hypocrites trade divinity
with symbolic rituals.
A land where obituaries and condolences
cost a lifetime's earnings.
A land where a gang of dropouts burnt a library,
demanding a script.
A land where illiterate grandparents shed spiritual tears
over the illicit affair of a god and his concubine.
A land where mongrels and swine debate upon
the wisdom to rule or serve.
A land where vision takes a back seat
and the cart pleads for progress to the reluctant horse.
A land where the sick politician prescribes antidotes to the sedated,
like the seasoned harlot who moans like a virgin.
A land where a poet wonders aloud,
though it's against the grain to ask:
'Who caused the Ripples?'

K. Satchidanandan

Acknowledgements

So many good people helped me unconditionally in the making of this book. I am very grateful to all of them. I desire for their love to live in this page forever. Therefore, I cannot take the risk of missing anyone by making a list of names here. They will understand me.

The burden of mistakes in this book rests on me alone.

Contents

About You

'When did you wake up?' you once asked.

The blind laughed in my heart, and
I fell in love.
A dream escaped, but your hairs
Darkened its path.

When we make love
I hear the sea roaring in your curls, and
Feel an animal on your skin.
In the needles of rain, eyes are missing,
And a burning river rushes out of your crevice.

While a cuckoo cries for moon drops,
Dawn comes with a yawn,
And the coconut tree bends to comb
Your dishevelled clouds while I
Search for my succumbed heart
In crumpled pillows.

I see you flying away,
And I drink mountains from a bottle
Of sunsets, thinking about you
Until I hear the moon
Moaning for a window.

Black

(Musuk)

Black was a thief
who stole anything
between pots and clothes.

Son of a pundit,
he became a thief and
humiliated the Brahmins.

I did not want to be a thief,
but we were friends,
Black and I.

All hated him,
but he surprised me
with his other colours.

We fell in love
with the same woman,
who loved him over me.

I spat venom
when Black walked past me
with her in his arms,
wearing my new shirt
I couldn't find the other day
sometime between noon and dusk.

Sad and defeated,
with vengeance nibbling on my heart,
I returned home late.

I found my shirt on the bed,
with a note from Black:
'Sorry! I'd to look clean for her.'

On a frozen January morning,
they found his body
hanging from a tree.

'Now he has paid for her,' said those
who hated him, but I heard
her tears saying, 'They killed him!'

I forgave him for the shirt and
his love for her,
and I still keep the shirt clean.

Musuk means 'black' in Manipuri.
He was a childhood friend; he died in 1974.

Invisible Man

I am your invisible man,
who is weary of revelations.

Warmth from a rub,
a cry, and the tremor
are all within sight except your love,
which remains defiant.

I drag a corpse
whose funeral
is kept at abeyance
until you see my face
every time you unbutton yourself
for your visible men.

Misfortune

My face, language, and colour say I'm a misfit
to live in your country or even be called your brother.
My father, teachers, and girlfriends too once said
I was misbegotten.
But my mother never thought so.

How I express myself to you is even more difficult
because mother taught me to be honest to myself.
Was it a mischance that I was born on a pallet without a midwife?
And everyone considered it a mother's duty to give the family a son,
and she did.

A thin, bony boy with sunken cheeks, who could have died of
tuberculosis at eleven,
I never attended school till the seventh standard.
My father was asked to bribe someone to admit me to a school, and
he did.
And he wanted me to become a doctor,
But inside me, I hated doctors.

Mother always cooked fresh vegetable soup with fish for me,
for father asked her to make me fit to absorb science.
I heard him complain to mother every night in bed about my weak
bones and
dull brain as if he had no part in me.
I began hating life in that place called home.
But one man saved me from my solitude.
My grandpa was my hero.

He taught me how to ride a bicycle.
He blew music in my ears through a flute.
He guided my fingers to touch flowers and nipples with respect.
He allowed me to think of love with purity while my father hit me
when I wrote
love on my geometry book. Since then I hated triangles.

One day, I asked grandpa about grandma
He looked at a cloud above the hills
for a long time and said: She was a good woman.'
I never asked the question again. My grandma was a bird who had
flown to the hills with a cloud.
But his mother, my great-grandma, was my grandma, a squirrel
who ate only bananas.
She lived two days beyond a hundred and died in her sleep with a
blade beneath her bedding,
its edge facing away from her body
as if protecting her from enemies.
And I thought she was a lady samurai.

How could this land be mine where I wasn't taught my letters?
But I love the river in front of our home,
which brought logs from the hills.
Every monsoon, its flood water turns our courtyard into a pond,
in which I began my rafting adventures on plantain-trunk floats
while homeless snakes swam alongside, escaping men and water.

And I never knew that I too will be escaping from you and your land
when I will be humiliated as a stranger among you.
To tell you the truth, I once hoisted your flag out of ignorant
allegiance.
Now I curse myself for having done that.
How elusive is the face of the enemy?
Shrapnel-shaped fish bone lodged in a wax model of a woman

tied all around by virgin threads was found nailed on a rafter of
our house.
And mother got sick, mad, and hysterical; she lost her identity in
sorcery.
She stopped cooking for me but added poison to my milk and
smiled at me while I was lifting the glass to my lips.
Suddenly, she slapped the glass away, and tears rolled down her
cheeks.
Her eyes embracing me, her birth pangs rang in my ears as if
she was delivering me in front of me one more time, and the soil
under her soles sweetened.
Who did that to her? No one knew.
But I can't forgive the history book you forced upon us, even as we
scratched
the ground to unearth roots of our tongue.
Who is responsible for my brother's disappearance?
I have forgotten how he looked like except the one I see in a picture
of him holding a toy car, his nose running and a few rice grains
sticking around
his mouth, imprisoned in a frame.

If you really want to know me, come closer behind me, and I will
break the mirror with a stone—and there you'll see me in my
worthlessness.
And you'll understand the mishap of broken faces.

Perfumes

Let him kiss me with kisses of his mouth—
for your love is better than wine.

Song of Solomon 1:2

Wicked wind hammering on doors and windows,
trying to storm in while we lay in a green bed,
my left hand under your head
and my right hand embracing you.
Your ebony breasts flapped like a pair of vanilla pods
from Madagascar,
slapping me with the sandy flames of Sahara.
You open your casket of perfumes,
a mysterious fumigation defying traditional smells,
blanketing us with misty fragrance, and I prepare
my burial in your arms, burning an aged incense
to prove my existence.
Rivers converging in your wild hips, and
I oar my dinghy with creaks of a dying wheel.

Do not be angered, my love, by the shrieks of a mocking bird,
for it too is calling its mate before the moon fades away.
We should be busy bathing our love
with spikenard sweats from my hills and
ylang-ylang juice from your beloved Comoros
washing your ruddy countenance

while your bewildered eyes reach a point of no return,
and I inhale the musky evaporation from your jar
overflowing with newborn perfumes.
My love, let us write poems with perfumed words
and scent the curses of veneering poets to venerate poetry.

Shipih's Journey

Forty-seven years old,
but he remains lost at eleven.
He smiles at dogs and people
with effortless honesty.
He rolls an iron ring and
follows the sun every day
along the Wah-Umkhrah.
Having been sired by an outsider,
everyone calls him Shipih, and
he cleverly hides a protest.
He attends no school
but raises a finger and
says 'Up yours' when provoked.
At dawn today,
Shipih and his wheel
wait for the sun to begin
another day's journey.
He talks to his metallic partner,
'Today, we will tail the sun
till we find the east,' and
they trail westwards under a coughing sky.

Wah-Umkhrah: a river in Shillong.
Shipih (Khasi): half of a rupee. An offspring of a Khasi mother
and a non-khasi father is often called a shipih.

Thynroit

(A Village in the Khasi Hills)

Sickly pine trees in tiny clusters
on balding hillocks with grey grass
fight a harsh battle for survival
against the bronchial suffocation
of dust storms stirred up from the ravaged road
that winds up to the village church,
where an elderly clergyman sleeps
every Sunday morning amidst fluctuating notes
of a choir of country girls.
The young pastor preaches gospel truths
in native dialect with some of his own sermons,
his mind, however, pondering
upon the cuisine he'll be savouring later
in homes of the faithful
who had been blessed with a good harvest
of potatoes and cabbages.
A middle-aged village drunk
shouts obscene warnings to a black bull
for molesting his wife's cow grazing nearby.
The village masseur sits on a rickety chair
and waits for city clients with broken limbs.
Screaming urchins in dirty red, blue, and pink gumboots
stampede on the dusty path to the crowded watershed
where their aunts and sisters wash smudged linens.

But when the sun sets behind the emptying hills
after the church doors have been locked
and the good book has been closed for the day,
a calm silence settles down on the village,
and the moon takes the shape of a clipped fingernail
while a dog howls at it in wolfish superstition.
Between echoes of mothers calling their children home,
Thynroit urges me to remember a village
in a faraway land I left behind.

A Cruise to the Past

Friends of the family say
that I inherited this obstinate habit
of chasing mice in my head
from my promiscuously adventurous grandpa,
who could live with ease in the cramped and babbling company
of my four grandmas under one roof!

He hated to live in confusion, and I dislike living in peace until
I find the needle in the haystack.
So driven by this genetic agitation,
I set out on a cruise downstream the Chindwin
in search of the lost folks who were spirited away
during the dreaded and infamous invasion and seven years'
devastation of my land by the Burmese in 1819.

Seated comfortably in the military patrol boat
generously provided by my old buddy, Col. Zaw Win,
a prominent string-puller of the ruling junta,
I could sense the stench of the leftover blood
on the cold breeze in my nostrils
through the waves churned by the razor-sharp blades of
the speeding boat's propeller, which reminded me of a king
who washed his bloody sword in this mighty river
a few centuries ago.
The soldier who was with me pointed his index finger
towards a row of pagodas on the left bank of the river and said,
'Look, we have reached the Sagain Division, where your king
signed the Treaty of Yandaboo on the 24th of February 1826.'

After nine gruelling hours, we reached the point
where the Chindwin meets the Irrawaddy and debarked
on the left bank, boarded a military jeep that was, once again a timely
help from the colonel, and drove towards Mandalay.
The twin white lions guarding the Mandalay hilltop pagoda
greeted me when I entered the city.
Then I received a footprint of an unknown smile,
which nudged me to a forbidden temptation.
In a red-light street of the city,
inside a karaoke bar filled with smoke from Burmese cigars
puffed by the nocturnal locals, I ordered a martini on the rocks
and sat down at a corner table.
A while later, a slim figure of a young Burmese woman
with a pretty face, wearing a golden sarong, darkened my table and said,
'*Mingalaba*, can I join you?'
I stood up, pulled out a chair for her
like a true Victorian gentleman
and replied, 'Be my guest,' and ordered a drink for her.
She smiled back bewitchingly and raised her glass,
and then she conjured a white lily out of nowhere, gave it to me, and said,
'Tonight, you can sleep with this flower and me for 1,000 kyat.'

Stunned by her audacity, I asked, 'Who are you?'
She replied, 'I am a teacher, times are bad now, I need the money.'
I looked at her eyes but couldn't find an answer,
and then I stood up,
counted 1,000 kyat, put it down on the table,
bent down, and kissed her
on the forehead. And I said, '*Ceizube*, I am sorry,' and walked out of
the godforsaken place into the streets,
looked up at the Milky Way,

shouted a four-letter word to someone up there, and headed for
my hotel.
In my room, I went down on my knees and said a prayer for her.

The following day, the high priest of the Meitei Brahmin colony
in Mandalay took me to Amarapura, a Meitei village on the banks
of Irrawaddy.
There, I mingled with my lost folks, told them stories
about the land
of their origin, heard their stories too, shared a few teardrops
with them,
and hugged the children, who couldn't speak the language of their
forefathers.
I thought I had found the needle.
That day, night came early.

After a wholesome dinner at the high priest's home,
I was struck by a thunderbolt when he said to me,
'My dear friend, please marry my daughter and take her back to
Manipur.'
While I was searching for an appropriate answer,
his daughter came out of the next room, looked at me, and said,
'Please accept my father's offer, I want to find my roots.'
I looked at them, said nothing, walked out of the house,
went back to my room, and cried like a baby,
not because of the father,
not because of the daughter, not because of the lost folks, and not
even for me, but for destiny.

On the third day, I climbed the hilltop pagoda,
meditated with a monk, facing the Irrawaddy in the horizon
overlooking the golf course.
When I asked about the military leader Gen. Than Shwe,
the monk's face became red with anger and he furiously replied,

'He is the incarnation of the devil, he even calls Daw Aung Suu Kyi
a neocolonial whore.'
I left the monk with his anger and climbed down the 1,070 stone
steps with a strange enlightenment in my mind.

On my way back, leaving behind the memories of my days
in the city of Mandalay, I visited the Kaungmudaw Paya Pagoda,
looked at the huge door frame,
and searched for the marks left on it
by another king's sword a few centuries ago.
I couldn't find any.

On the other side, at Moreh, the Indian border town,
I was frisked and barked at by BSF soldiers, who took away
everything I brought from across the border.
That night, unable to sleep on the bug-ridden bed in the
run-down hotel room and haunted by the howling of the generator
behind the building, I heard the voice of the priest's daughter again.
I looked up at the ceiling fan, which was struggling to uproot itself
out of the concrete slab, and murmured aloud to myself,
'Sweetheart, today, I am as rootless as you are!'

Mingalaba (Burmese): greetings.
Ceizube (Burmese): thank you.

And the Train Leaves without Her

On that hot summer day when she boarded the train,
it slumped in despair.
Its engine screamed while it rolled away with my love and
her unborn child on a journey to the white mountains.
I smiled at her broody face in my doomed attempt to bid
a no-worry farewell.

Her folks and my folks said,
'You are not rich enough to make love,' for we were
careless flames desperately in love.

Her absence haunted me through insomniac nights,
and my anxious prayers to indifferent gods,
who hid behind shady temple doors, faded away
with disappearing shadows of an autumn night,
which did not howl but gave birth to an enfeebled dawn.

Daybreak brought injurious winds, which mocked me
with such fierce jibes: 'Your invincible groin's pride had caused
a lily to shed its dimples, and look at you—a malicious drunk.'
I knew no star will be named after me,
but I swore to stain the sky with my blood and
discourage conspirators from transforming our love
into a weighty theme of city gossip
before a choppy sea of rumours drowns all dreams.

Winter arrived with its dazzling snow,
burdening the leafless branches and paralyzing the streams
of our hills.
A sharp blade of bitter ice slashed my heart,
and no suture could hold the edges together.

Fortunately, the knife in the wind
missed my throat, for my woman left behind a scarf
scented in her surreal perfume, which cast a protective fog
and puzzled the hooded executioner.

Clattering hooves of spiteful hags trampled my soul, and
no priest in spotless surplice with his holy waters
could cleanse the anguish of my loneliness.
Astonishingly, a train stops today, and she disembarks
with a little boy holding her fingers, his deep-blue eyes
looking for answers.
She smiles, and I gratefully smile back,
no longer a non-believer,
and the train leaves without her.

Debts

I owe so many.
And they've become overweight.
I can't carry them.
Whenever I returned home
in the dead of midnight,
the debt I owe my mother,
who waited up without eating.
When I lay in a drunken stupor at the wayside,
the obligation I owe the mongrel
who licked away sweat from my flyblown face.
The due I owe the neighbourhood
for not beating me black and blue
for the peeks I took as she bathed
when Memchoubi was a virgin.
And although I spent the night at Chandramukhi's,
the burden I owe my wife
when she pretended that she didn't know
even as I lied.
The debt I owe my son
for simply yielding to my deceit
because it wasn't enough for a bottle
when he longed for a toy train.
And when I returned
after a long spell,
the debt I owe
the fields and pastures I'd forgotten
for telling me I've reached home.
How will I pay my debts to all

for loving me in excess?
Mulling over this, I'm also searching
for a deep-rooted tree
to crucify myself.

Translated by Robin S. Ngangom from the poet's Manipuri poem
'Laman'.

Smells

*(This poem is dedicated to Assam's renowned
singer Deepali Borthakur and artist Neel Pawan Baruah.)*

I smelt milk in my room
when she entered wearing a cloud
borrowed from the sky-blue curtain.
Her breasts were wet with milk,
eager to wean an infant poem,
but I wasn't ready to grow.
She then melted,
her milk with the smell of
a wet crow flying off with a broken wing
from the sunset ripples of the river, her lover!
In my hills, breasts and udders have roots,
and milk smells like earth. 'How could I
contain your milk, which flies?' I told her
in anxiety.

Echo of a call from a bedroom, a fallen voice,
that I heard the other day in her land,
asking her bearded brush to paint her music
on a fading canvass, made me whisper
a wish: a dream walk on her milky way!
A father-to-be who lived next to her alley too
was kneading dusts of steel to mould a womb
with seeds of his love in it.
That too was a dream which smelt milk!
Who said I've shelved my dreams?
But with what net should I catch the smell of

a raven with murky black feathers drenched in tears?
She shouldn't have forgotten the smells
when she brought in the flowers. Restless smells!

When I made love with her in my dreams,
her sweat smelt a rice field
which she once tilled with a dry nib.
Her cry too was impatient,
impatient like a breeze struggling to
become a storm!
Hastily spent breaths which left me exhausted
had mingled with the yellow wishes
she wore before shedding them on a mustard field in her village,
seeds scattered for oil. Fiery smell!
And like a purple jacaranda flower
which fell on dewy morning grass,
she lay beside me in accomplished dreams.
She rolled the *ma-kyllain* I brought
from the hills and completed the intricate ritual
with a slide on her wet tongue and then
lit it with a flame from a leftover passion, and dusty
smoke darkened my room while a rustic smell
took shelter between her narrow breasts.
And I yearned to own a cigarette shop,
where she'll come and review her face on a
mirror hung upside down,
her cosmetics to please drunk clients.
Sometimes, leisurely chats between us when business
is down, hers and mine!
And then, smell of cigarette butts and
rotting hearts will make us cry—bloody smell!
We should have waited for another
Rongali Bihu to weave a scarlet *gomosha*
and the bleeding—the prejudicial sacrifice!

But the hope that he, the grey brush, paints
on empty cigarette boxes and soiled newspapers
a symphony of a cuckoo and her lover,
a fragrance called the smell of love,
transcending territorial insecurity of
man and his filthy habits—the bad smells!

Ma-kyllain (khasi): locally cut tobacco to roll into cigarettes.
Rongali Bihu (Assamese): spring festival of Assam.
Gomosha (Assamese): indigenous towel of Assam.

History of Our Rice

A feeble aroma lingering on my tongue
becomes a poem, a poem about our rice.
Hidden and hurting me
with memories, history of our rice
in my mouth.

Born with misfortune
of not knowing our rice, my children;
our rice is gone, like
the winds that teased them
when they ripened last.

I, born in the heydays
of my father's father, who
planted myths in our rice fields, was blessed
by growing up with his story of rice,
my only bedtime story,
of how our neighbour with weak eyesight, whose
rice fields too bordered ours, sowed
seeds of *Phouren Amubi* in our fields—a tale
of mistaken beds.
Fearing humiliation in the hands of his arrogant sons,
he disclosed to my grandpa his blunder
in hushed conspiracy, pleading for help.
A shrewd peacemaker, my old man's father
sowed seeds of *kakcheng phou*
in his neighbour's fields.

The rice fields, like dancers with golden earrings,
swayed like drunken lovers
in December's shivering air. And
the friends—grandpa and his
neighbour—only laughed, hoping for
a good harvest.
And then they exchanged looks
when wrong aromas came
from misplaced kitchens, and
their children shook heads in disbelief.

There were other neighbours too,
less fortunate though, who planted
taothabi phou and *huikap phou,*
lesser species of rice which grew floating on their
ever-drowned rice fields, roots exiled from soil.
They too had stories of friends, joy, and fate,
bittersweet memories of someone like me
somewhere in a faraway village.

But I still say those were the days,
days of our rice and their aromas
soaked in love and brotherhood,
with smells of earth and smoky wine
fermented with stealthy kisses
of ripening virgins who winked at stars
on half-moon nights.
Our rice is gone, mutated,
to feed the gods in the heavens.
Maybe the days will soon come
of rice which bleeds friends and neighbours
over words spoken in haste.
Hearts too will become
dry grains crushed between

rocks and hard ground no plough can explore.
What shall I leave behind
for my grandchildren, a bedtime story
of poisoned love of a vanishing tribe,
whose people no longer live on rice
but on bullets carved with names
of their unborn children?

I won't be surprised
to find a frozen teardrop of my mother
with a grain of our rice hidden in it
beside a bullet with my name on it.

Rife with hostility,
roots dare not grow in caking mud, and
we no longer see startled catfish
and lazy earthworms when we walk
through young rice fields.

Perhaps we should plant guns in our fields,
and hopefully bullets will become rice and
we'll die without bleeding, a nobler way
to end the history,
for we too will cease to exist, like our rice, and
we needn't knead a *chengphu* or knit a *meruk*,
for no sty will hurt our eyes any longer.

Phouren Amubi: a very aromatic indigenous rice variety of Manipur which is now extinct.
Kakcheng Phou: a small grain variety of Manipuri rice with a distinct aroma which is also extinct.
Taothabi Phou: a cheaper quality rice of Manipur; this species grows floating on water.

Huikap Phou: floating-rice species like *Taothabi;* it is called huikap (*hui* means 'dog', and *kap* means 'cry') because of its hardness when cold that even dogs cry while chewing it.

Chengphu: earthen pot used to store rice.

Meruk: small basket to measure rice; Meiteis cover their infected eye with meruk and throw it backwards before crossing the threshold and entering the house, never looking back—a superstitious remedy practised to cure sty.

Is This My Home?

Memories only live here.
But even the shadows of my childhood
had been moved.

I bring you here to show my toys.
But even the cradle walks bent at the waist,
a rusty toy car lodged between her wrinkles,
a tattered doll with a *potloi* with faded colours
sleeping in its back seat.

My index finger wants to point for you the space where
my room was, somewhere among torn-down pillars
of an old house lying as a defeated general.
But aroma of honeysuckle from the mark left by a trellis
on a fallen wall still haunts the air.

The man who fathered me sits in his old headmaster's clothes,
and his face once again has a teacher's authority
while you bow to him in memory of a forgotten teacher
of your village's school.
And I feel proud of the man blessing you now.
He too is proud to meet you,
for both of you were taught by the same masters.
I am glad you become his friend instantly.
I wish this is always my home.
But something is missing in this crafted friendliness.
We are all actors assigned with our specific roles.

I as a good lover and a son.
You as a jubilant bird that has found a new cage.
My father as a man who at last could show off his nothingness
when he justifies the statute disqualifying mother
from sitting alongside him on the same mat in public.
Your friend as a Good Samaritan, silently enjoying the irony.
My mother smiling joyfully on her final satire
when she lights the cigarette I bought for her in public.

And the act completes with the ultimate dance
of a shrew's broom sweeping away my footprints
from the ruins of my grandfather's dreams
while my brother remains possessed by her spells.

I hope you understand me
when I hold your hand and leave the place for good
beneath your wings covered with yellow pollen from a mustard field
in search of a home where I'll never ask:
'Is this my home?'

Potloi (Manipuri): bridal dress of the Meiteis.

Bardoishikhla

(Wind–water woman)

She comes back home
For the first time after her wedding.
Her mother rearranges her mirror and comb,
For she will review her curls.

In the manner she liberated them in a storm
Once upon a time.
But she sits leaning on an aged tree in Lawkyntang,
Reluctant to go, mending rugged fig trunks for orchids
Which will arrive with April's first drizzles to shine

The green shadows with swinging lamps.
She looks happy, but her eyes are nervous
In fear of wounds envious of her pain.
I am happy too, for she dances around the trees

In a vibrant dress, painting the woods red.
I hear wind, boys in haste to announce their arrival.
I hear another wind, girls chasing their future after the boys.
I hear a noise, windy mothers calling back their daughters

Lest dreams become tears.
I hear an anxious wind, uncles grumbling ceaselessly,
Persuading their nieces to stay away from boys.
Where are the fathers?

They are drinking in a bush
Behind a witchy old oak on which an ailing squirrel guffaws.
A stream leaps between mossy rocks with grunts
Of protest against the garbage—the drinking fathers.

Desperate to meet her daughter, her mother sends
Her little brother, a bird calling out her name after
Intervals of five swaying treetops.
The winds return, no longer boys or girls

The drunken fathers become sad winds.
Engulfed by the chaotic madness, they lost their daughters.
I see and become a walking monolith dragging vows
On a carpet of dry leaves whimpering under my feet,
Begging for rain, which brings sleep.

Bardoishikhla (Bodo root word) or *Bordoisila* (Assamese): It is a stormy wind usually occurring in Assam at the time of Bohag Bihu, a festival welcoming spring; it is also believed in folklore of Assam that a woman who had gone to become a wife comes back to her parents' home to reminisce her past, and after the festivities, she then goes back calmly.

Lawkyntang (Khasi): a sacred grove in the Khasi Hills; the Khasis believe God dwells in it.

For Some Reasons

For some reasons, I doubted my father
for his intentions of making me while he made love.

For some reasons, I doubted my mother
for her justifications of marrying my father.

For some reasons, I doubted my birth
for purposes mysterious even as I avoided revelations.

For some reasons, I doubted my land's history for its
existence in a country where my citizenship is questioned.

For some reasons, I doubted God for being centrifugal
in identifying our inclusiveness within an exclusive culture.

These snarls have become faces of the ghosts
of my brothers crying in exile, denying the masks

handed out to resemble a people on the other side of a river
we always cross with cynical apprehensions in fear of rejection

for some reasons . . . !

Fear

That night was endless passion, and I
raised an army in my heart to protect you from me.
Stones that I wanted to load my sling with to kill the giant
pounding on my heart, I quarried out from a half-bitten moon.
But abundant were your breasts with temptations,
your ancestral inheritance: the bust of Venus.
Armless but dripping with intrinsic yearnings
carved out of white marble, they embraced me,
a hummingbird in a mulberry bush, and
I sailed with squeaking oars.

You've learnt to shed tears inside, accomplished
the art of banishing fear, fear of love, so that
your eyes remain dry while you cry
behind closed doors somewhere.

Night was floating with us, the only people
in love, touching each other on harmless limbs,
a defeat I intended to treasure forever and walk
proudly, for I've given you no shame.
It takes two to sin, the covetousness, but
we changed its name: sleeplessness.

Your journey is long, longer than the road.
Mine short, shorter than a wish.
But I was the cave in which you spent the night
when your road petered out on a timeless walk.
You slept face down, your face hidden in the shadow

of your curly nest, and I couldn't know what was on it—
a smile or a cry!
And the fear was cruel, crueller than a sting.
But I accepted the defeat by silencing the promptings,
and you slept without dreams.

Needles of rain fell on a puddle, became infant circles
which died after three tiny ripples, and my heart skipped
a beat for the bubble we broke that night,
which was almost a placenta.
And I agreed when you said orchids aren't parasites,
they only take shelter in a tree.
But, my love, they became a crowd, and a leaf which fell
on one autumn's morning didn't know its part of the tree
and died a fugitive.
So I waged war against that fear and succeeded
in protecting our love from becoming an ordinary happening.
My sword, honesty, struck, and a desire died with a yell.

My Stray Thoughts

Caged in the twilight of my life,
my middle-class soul yearns to fly.
Wings of my stray thoughts
surge me like a sudden breath.

Berries among thorns,
sweet wine squeezed
became gooseberry between lovers.

A ray of sunlight
exposes a dusty room.
A word of truth calms a storm of lies.

Walked through *Kabaw Valley*
met an old teak tree with ears of mushroom,
drops of history dripping from its leaves.

A monk, tired of paedophilia,
left monastery and celibacy,
fathered offspring of his own.

Mahogany sunset,
shadows of homecoming sparrows on the setting sun,
a stray bullet hits a nest somewhere in the east.

A bullet cracks,
a lifeless body slumps,
startles the chirping birds,

politicians slumber on.

The highlander poet says,
'Write a line a day,
uncage words from the dictionary.'

A poet demands applause,
a parrot mimics his poetry,
he falls in love with the bird.

Strode knee-deep in snow,
scaled Mt Lhotse below Mt Everest.
'Boy! Go Back Home,' said the noble peak.
A chopper hovered above me.

A spot on my back,
I couldn't reach to scratch.
Itches the most—that damned spot.

Unable to fly across cloistered yew forests,
my aged soul falls on flames of *nahar* trees,
and my charred heart joins autumn's falling leaves
while my stray thoughts descend on an arid spring.

Kabaw Valley: a valley of teak trees on the Indo-Myanmar border,
which was a part of Manipur before it was gifted to Burma by India.

Nahar: it is a tree native to the north-east of India; its young leaves
have the colour of flames.

A Land of Ripples

A land where guns are no longer fired in anger
but in deceitful dreams.
A land where people starve for a peaceful recipe
till they are no longer hungry.
A land where hypocrites trade divinity
with symbolic rituals.
A land where obituaries and condolences
cost a lifetime's earnings.
A land where a gang of dropouts burnt a library,
demanding a script.
A land where illiterate grandparents shed spiritual tears
over the illicit affair of a god and his concubine.
A land where mongrels and swine debate upon
the wisdom to rule or serve.
A land where vision takes a back seat
and the cart pleads for progress to the reluctant horse.
A land where the sick politician prescribes antidotes to the sedated,
like the seasoned harlot who moans like a virgin.
A land where a poet wonders aloud,
though it's against the grain to ask:
'Who caused the Ripples?'

Anxiety

My heart is a schism
It has always been a stuttering gait
Having burnt roses in your garden
Every time your tears tried to cleanse
The indifference of the other me
And I feel its disability when I begin
My days with mornings without you
Your shadow's rule on it
Becomes more ruthless when
Slow raindrops fall carrying gestures
Of your mischievous smiles
In translucent wet prisons
How I wish every day to wade
In the swamp of your hairs
Cut a reed and blow a precipitous tune
To awake the dots of your sleeping rabbits
Or surrender myself to a blackbird's beak
Pecking at a cloud for milk
While you spread your tresses
Sprawling on the snow of your dreams
Making my existence spurious
In this place where winds whisper poetry
To moist pine needles
Multiplying my anxiety of your absence
In my journey through deserts of wrinkled sheets.

Durga

The adorations ended on another rainy day, and
drowning idols left drunken devotees
in venting devotion with their faint chanting.

'Stone the bitch,' they shouted.
Bottles and stones were cast at a woman lying dead-still
behind a tree.
I tiptoed above the wild heads,
saw her bloodless face, and I murmured, 'Durga.'

I once knew her, a woman who dreamed of becoming a goddess,
and she was always a goddess
whenever we warmed cold nights together.

An altar boy behind me cursed and threw a stone
clouting her dead-on on the forehead, and
I heard a moan leaving her lips.

The last time I saw her
was in a madhouse, but she left it and
had been walking the streets, singing strange songs,
I was told.

On that religious day, she committed a blasphemy:
stealing a sari from a sinking idol and
wrapping it around her denuded body and dancing like a goddess.

I saw the blood, and she cried, 'Mother.'

I abhorred the idols and the dirty river,
bit my cowardly lips, and walked away from the scene.

I looked back at an idol and remembered:
the goddess was actually born in a mound on the courtyard of a
whore!

Durga: a Hindu goddess.

I Am Not Even a Dream

Since I left the silence of my mother's womb,
I have stopped dreaming.
During that umbilical slumber,
She fed me with exceeding love unconditionally
That I now remain only a heart, without sleep and dreams.
This scarcity of dreams in your book of laws, scorching
Life, air, earth, and other elements, has put me in poverty of warm pillows.
How badly I need dreams to know your act of substitution nailed on a tree.
Don't the landlord's hound and the street mongrel
Enjoy a common dream for a stout bone? Why am I deprived?
I've been trying to become a dream while frogs leap into sounds of midnights, hoping
Rugged rocks will slumber with dreams of becoming ferns.
But your universe is an insomniac void in which I fumble with fragments
Of dreams, which are stolen when I wake up.
Love that crucified you
Has eyes more than pineapples, and without stars in my eyes,
My heart's gaze is dead whenever I look at the man in the mirror.
You once asked, 'Can you drink from my cup?' Cupful of transgressions!
Could one do that without candles melting dreams in your altar's darkness?
I must fall sick now with fever to catch
A dream and empty my nights on your wounds, for
I am not even a dream,
Which could follow a crow's flight.

It Makes No Difference

It makes no difference that I have the heart of a butcher, which quakes with nonchalance while his hands habitually tremble when the cleaver cracks the bones, or when I find two women live inside the woman whom I love, one consoling the other while the other kneads vengeance. It makes no difference when the flag no longer flutters if asked to in a strange anthem or which country I belong to, for no poetry owns my land. It makes no difference what greying hair means, for death is no longer a certainty. It is only a day in the calendar. It makes no difference how old I am when falling leaves turn into butterflies, urging autumn to fly without hesitation. And how can I hate my enemy when I see him kissing his child before he leaves home to fight me? Ever since I chased the poem playing mischief in your eyes and began to draw lines on the sands of your river while I ran my fingers in your unkempt hair and squandered my soul, I haven't stopped muttering, 'Where am I?' But it makes no difference how dark shadows are as I finally close my eyes to the sun. It makes no difference that my land is not a nation as we strive for sovereignty in frivolous valour. The truth is, we are lessons short of patriotism. And when my doctor reveals my blood is sick with sweetness, it makes no difference of what flavour was the blood we shed on defeated battles. Therefore, it makes no difference what bitter reasons we seek to justify the hate we practise. As I am now incurably sweetened, it makes no difference what weapons my enemies sharpen, for I have gathered honey. It makes no difference what my heart murmurs as it is a little shy of being remnant. It makes no difference to my mother, who is in menopause, why a *chek-cheki* keeps wailing on the dry eucalyptus tree in our backyard after my comrades have died in the haemorrhage of rebellion.

Makes no difference whether you despise my craft as long as soft winds sough through tall bamboo when I recite it repeatedly under moonless skies. I once heard a little girl reciting a poem of identity on the country's Independence Day; her first line was 'Where am I? Where am I? In this crowd of strangers!' I wish I could tell the little girl: 'We are neither at home nor on a journey, but in a place called error, wearing borrowed masks.'

Chek-cheki (Assamese): it is a small bird native to Assam; it is believed when a woman hears its calls, she understands her menstruation is about to happen.

My Wife Is Away to the Mountains

My wife is away to the mountains, visiting her folks.
She left the windows guarded
with curtains made of her *jainsem*.

Last night the moon peeped in through the protective embroidery
but failed to seduce me as I was secured in the possessive perfume
of my love exuding from the wilful drapes.

There are times between midnight and dawn, I dream of an open
harbour
swallowing waves of salty ships into her inflamed mouths.

But in the morning, when the north wind flutters my wife's curtains,
I pity the drowned pirates in their defeats on that adulterous night
of stormy lusts.

Then I realize they needed a dedicated poet to calm the storms,
who can sprinkle the sacrificial blood of his circumcised words
on the cruel crevices of the wild seas.

Neighbours visit with ritualistic inquiry about my solitude and
well-being,
but their keep-watch concerns reveal through cleverly concealed
blushes,
reminding me of the wiles of threatened wives in tales told on the
moors.

Before dark clouds solicit the sleeping owl,

before an aged crow curses me with yellow teeth,
I ought to rush up the mountains to bring her back home before time
shuts away all the days of my life in superseded calendars.

My wife is away to the mountains, visiting her folks.

Jainsem: a dress worn by Khasi women.

My Wife Is Back from the Mountains

My wife is back from the mountains.
She brings along snow with her, and tonight
I too will become a mountain's heart.
Her mere presence has silenced the presumption
of all the mice ransacking our home
while she was away in the mountains.
Even the yellow-teethed hags greet her
with smiles pure as January rain.
My wife smiles mysteriously, and I, with my
mooning, believe nothing is amiss.
But in spite of all the possible storms
which might have been brewing up in the mountains
for which I may pay the price one day, she remains
the only chord with which my heart quivers.

No man has ever understood the mystery
although all have sailed on salty thighs,
only to be drowned in orgasmic thirst.
But tonight, when the moon sits high and two birds
keep chirping till late night and my wife cooks for me
the recipes she learnt from the mountains,
I feel myself blessed to be loved by a woman
whose gifts surpass all expectations of a scheming lover.
I was born to move on from one discovery to another,
but when I break bread with my wife tonight
once again amidst sleepy pines in our hills,
I finally cast anchor in her enfolding arms.

My wife is back from the mountains.

Prisoner

I

While the walls looked at us

What you took from me was yours
A teardrop in your inflamed eyelids
And what I returned you was
A little raindrop on a plum

As we embraced
Our hearts became wine leaking from a barrel
Staining the marble bed
With grapes softly becoming your nipples

Our eyes closed looking for dreams
Your dream rowed a boat towards a terracotta sunset
Mine shyly hid in the folds of your armpit
A cloud darker than a cave fell
And scared your yearnings

And I found myself locked in your curls
Pleading for shackles
My mistress, my seductress
Please throw the keys away

II

Talking to the walls

Of late, I have acquired the uncommon habit
Of talking to the walls about you
Standing alone at the centre of our bedroom
The bricks are all ears
While my envy of them dies in silence
For they have heard more of you

But I grind my teeth with a cruel grin
My eyes writing graffiti of a thirsty sword
On their square faces

And I tell them how we give birth to seasons
In our nightly symphony of touches
And brewing of fever in the thirst of fireflies
We make colours: purple, yellow, and the sky
And give our arrivals names of seasons

When you fly high, closing your eyes
It is spring
When you soar to the clouds, eyes wide open
With insane pupils, it is monsoon
And it is autumn
When you burst open a bubble with my age in your eyes
Staring distantly at me with your age on your lips
And when I wait for your nibbling to end
Holding back wild fires, burying my face into your neck
I call it summer

Finally when all the seasons are drowned
In salty tides of sweating limbs
Suddenly a hurricane sucks in the darkness
Spinning the ceiling
And the walls are without corners
Lifting us up on the hammock of a crescent moon
Your lost eyebrow
And our souls become intertwined rivers
Twisted by yellow storms from ravaged mustard fields
We call it Bardoishikhla

And when morning sends in a ray of light
Falling on your face still sleeping with a smile
And all seasons come to rest beneath your eyelashes
Gently rubbing in baby dreams into your eyes and then
Pulling up the fur quilt over us, I call it winter
While talking to the walls with defeated faces

Bardoishikhla: It is a word from the language of the Bodo tribe of
Assam, a state in the North-east of India. It is the root word of
Bordoisila, an Assamese word indicating a storm that comes every
spring before Bohag Bihu, a festival of the Assamese people. And
it is believed to be a woman who comes to her mother's home in
spring and goes back to her husband's home after the festivities
are over.

Superstition

We once had a papaya tree
on our garden's edge near the gate.
My mother planted it with fingers of love.
'You have to remove the small black seeds
before you eat the orange flesh,'
she told me while watering the plant.

The tree flowered
but failed to bear fruits.
My mother was anxious about the tree
and its fruitless future.
One sunny morning,
I saw her dressing the tree's trunk
with a piece of fabric torn from her old *Phanek*.
She believed the tree was a man, and
she had to change its sex for it to bear fruits.
I told my friends about it,
and we laughed, mocking superstition.
A season later, the tree flowered again
and bore a boom of fruits, surprising me
and my friends deliciously.
Since then, I left superstition alone.

Phanek: a typical sarong worn by Manipuri women.

Wet Curls

Wet curls
begging a wish
to touch them.
But for the mist,
white wool over eyes.

We saw
the haze went up
the gorge,
stroking the pines of Mawkdok,
and desperate
to hold your hand, I
kept the commandment.
What shall I do in heaven now
without your moist locks?

Pears blossomed
in pure white detachment,
but you took their pictures,
and I preferred to trap
your wayward ways in my fingers.
What shall I do with blossoms
if I can't fasten them to your hair?

Camellia flowers in flames
burned our eyes in the evening,
the western horizon cremating
the past
where we could have been.

Mawkdok: a beautiful tourist spot on the way to Cherapunjee,
Meghalaya.
Nohkalikai: a waterfall at Cherapunjee (fourth highest in the world).

A Piece of Advice for the Enemy

You can kill the poet but not the poem,
For what is written remains written.
The poet must die if the poem should live,
And if you want to stop the revolution,
The poet must be silenced.
For his words might raise a storm, and
In hearts and veins, blood will stir.
Where are your soldiers? Summon a firing squad.
The poet must be shot to save your army.
But do not put a wall behind him,
For his blood will splatter graffiti on it,
And before you could wipe, you'll fall in love with poetry.
The poet will breathe again; his babbling
Will be heard in the roiling streams of your hills and
Valleys, and you'll be enslaved.
Exile the poet if you can't kill him but confiscate his pen,
For with it he can turn insane.
Even if you could kill the poet, remember, don't let his
Blood spill, for it will turn into ink, and you'll be drowned.
And even you, a colonial offshoot, will mouth poetry,
Infected by his madness, even as your lungs suffocate.
With that vision of indignant displeasure waiting for you
On the sea's bed salted with blood from my brothers,
You've let ruthlessly over years of grief while mother
Spent years stretching her eyes to see her children return.

Autumn's Sweet Hurting

First day of autumn,
far more sacred almost
than my own birthday.
For on this day,
a long time ago, I fell in love with
a breeze falling from your tresses.

Each year when this day comes around,
I draw the well-sealed cork from a jar
and let the lamps burn till dawn
while I raise a hundred toasts
in memories of springs and summers.

Autumn is a fiction
until you live in it, and
it is too late to relearn seasons
once they set in.
But once in a while,
a few young leaves fall with dry ones
and ask questions to old ferns like me
about shapes and sizes of love,
grafting spring dreams on grey trees.

You deemed it sin
to hope for what is not allowed in fall,
when it pours out harvests and
short numb days recur.

But you'll not stop me from revelling on this day,
wearing a lively mask of spring,
which tolerates sky, rain, and my doorstep
while hurting me.

Endoscopy

While the lens man was busy
Discovering my gastric landmarks,
I looked up to a square sky through an oversized window,
A colonial leftover.
I squinted one of my eyes, pinched by no fewer than four gloves:
Three on my head and one on my face,
Covering half of my other eye.
And the sky, though square in shape, looked spectacular
When seen through warm tears.
A heavy cloud sailed across and
Vanished beyond the folded borders, then I saw
A falcon in the blue frame, with a picture of my woman in its claws,
And it flew away, beating its wings triumphantly.
I struggled to cry out in vain, for
There was a snake in my throat.
Bird shit hit the window glass.
The lens man pulled out his one-eyed snake, and
The gloves too released me and turned themselves
into white aprons with impish eyes.
Before I walked out of the wretched room,
I looked back and smiled,
For the undertakers and their snake
Didn't know I had stolen a poem from them
Which opened for me a door of utterance of my love
To my woman waiting outside,
Whose gentleness no bird can spirit away.

I Won't Walk on It!

'I won't walk on it!' says
the toddler, my niece.

She is afraid to tread on the land,
our ancestral acres now
reduced to a mossy courtyard.

She disowns the strange ground,
for it is yet to be tiled.

Her tender soles paddle on marbled floors,
chasing echoes of jingling anklets, and
stop at the edge where the soil begins,
like I hesitate in fear of a prayer's uncertainty
amidst randomly pointed rifles when
I set out for a day's affairs.
The road that leads to the market,

I won't walk on it!

Lazarus's Onward Journey

My friend
Lazarus of Bollongre died
in an accident.

He shook it more than twice
when he peed on the fence of Pundit Nehru Park,
and it cost him his life when a truck
rammed him from behind.

All of us,
his bereaved friends, knew
he wasn't Lazarus of Bethany, and
none of us a carpenter either.

But we shouted at the morgue's door,
'Lazarus, come forth,' beatified by barrels
of *bitchi* we drank in mourning.

At his funeral
two days later, we buried him
with pomp and gaiety.

His coffin rested on our shoulders
on the way to the cemetery, and we carry
the fond scars till this day.

His soul
rested for a while at Balpakram,
and he washed his feet in the black pool.

We hung chunks of smoked meat around the ancient rock,
food for his onward journey, and we shouted again,
'Lazarus, go forth.' And he left for his eternal home, and
we raised our glasses one more time for the road.

Bollongre: a village in Garo Hills of Meghalaya.
Bitchi (Garo): local rice beer.
Balpakram: an ancient holy spot of the Garos, believed to be a
temporary resting place for souls before departing for their eternal
resting place, now a tourist spot.

Rain Dance

My mother puts on her royal attire
to do the rain dance of a princess,
but her feet are barren,
for it no longer rains like before.

Years ago, I watched mother dance,
her fingers plucking moon petals
and dropping them on my sleepy eyelids
while I laughed in pleasure
on iridescent nights in a land of dreams.

We could hear father reciting faraway verses
in his bedroom; his words stepped out
to the porch and joined mother
in her dance with the moon.

Today, I stop mother in her attempt to dance
under a dark sky of gunpowder smoke
and in the company of drunk shadows
of dry mango trees wafting in wild winds,
and she gives up quietly.

An explosion shatters the silence,
and mother wriggles her feet,
her heels grinding the burning earth.

She looks at me with wet eyes and says,
'Son, it thunders, let me dance,' and
I see only the raindrops in her eyes.

But it no longer rains like before
in the land where mother lives.

Sweet Little Sohiong

Sweet little Sohiong!
You should cut loose from your *Mei's* arms,
for you are now ripe for a man.
Do you sleep while I expire for you
the whole night long?
I've seen you sleeping before
in your Mei's lap,
like a drop of blood clinging to a cut vein,
but you are now a heart that should be awake,
dancing to liquid melodies of love
the whole night long.
After friends disperse, when jars are drained,
and enemies return to their anvils, sharpening
blunted swords thirsty for my blood,
with what arrow should I wound my foes
unless your red wine intoxicates my feeble heart?
We all must bury our bones,
yours and mine, on different nights,
for an old song separates us between now and never.
Ocean's hands touch your dunes clumsily;
my shabby indiscretion for which they exiled me
was only the sound of a Latin poem
which mocked your Mei's cruel humour.
My mirror looks back sadly,
impelling me to bloody brawls over fairy tales
until I scatter three handfuls of earth and hurry away.

Sweet little Sohiong!
I'm telling you one more time,
you are now ripe for a man; fall and bleed sweetly
before your Mei's leaves become venomous.

Sohiong: indigenous cherry fruit of the Khasi hills with blood-red
juice.
Mei: 'mother' in Khasi.

A Poet on the Loose

A bearded regal poet once appeared
in the streets of our hills.

He fantasized in amoral desire
that his lost lover could be found
between coniferous thighs.

He even mistook the eyes of a cab driver
in a rear-view mirror
to be of his elusive lover.

He scaled the slopes,
looking for lovers, wanting them to betray him
one more time.

A soldier glanced at him;
the poet manufactured a rape as though
he bore the weight of a bull amok in venery.

He was tired,
but he sipped my wine as if
he was the pope tasting perfectly chilled Chianti.

I thought he was drowned in queer wine,
for his face became ambiguous with
the colour of the pinkest rose.

He then rose and wrote a poem
on a wall of the youth hostel room
about my ugly liver, and
I realized how lost he was
in that wilderness of self-worshipping love.

In the Hills of Seven Huts

In the hills of seven huts,
where *war* is either a place or surname,
and dreams are translated into numbers,
and a number became a gambler's sad song,
I found God breathing through the pine trees.

Orchards in the hills shivered in winter's palms,
golden oranges plucked for city bazaars,
a young leaf wanted to go along,
discontented orange tree held it back.

A fleeting rainbow across Noh-Ka-LiKai,
a glimpse of her precious final steps,
before she became a waterfall.

Twangs of hammer on hot iron,
a dagger hissed in a bucket of water,
Mylliem's blacksmiths keep their tradition throbbing.

Mylliem's giant boulders,
memoirs of the great earthquake,
'We were cast out recklessly,'
says a mossy stone.

Sunday morning in the church,
a pair of long legs walked past a pew,
a clergyman sighed in agony.

Christmas in Shillong,
roast turkey on the table,
rush of stampeding shoppers,
merchants carol their way to the bank.

A dog swallowing the moon,
beating of empty tins, chasing the dog away,
I became a lunar-eclipse drummer in Shillong's hills.

I went down on my knees,
and asked God for my biblical rib,
and I found her snoring gently beside me,
in the hills of seven huts.

The Khasi Hills in the state of Meghalaya is also known as the land of seven huts.

War (Khasi): There is a place called *war* in Khasi hills on the Indo-Bangladesh border. *War* is also a surname of the Khasis.

Noh Ka LiKai (Khasi): A beautiful waterfall in Cherapunjee. A folk tale of the Khasis tells that Likai was a poor woman whose baby daughter was butchered and cooked by her drunk second husband while she was away working in the fields, and she ate the meat (her daughter's flesh) later in supper. She found the child's fingers in the basket of betel leaves and Arica nuts, and having realized what she had done, she committed suicide by jumping off a cliff. There came up a waterfall, and it was named after her—*noh ka likai*, meaning 'where Likai jumped'.

Mylliem (Khasi): a village in the Khasi Hills of Meghalaya.

Shillong: capital of Meghalaya; an enchanting hill station in the North-East of India.

Peeling Tattoos

Since you bring up the subject of tattoos,
come closer, let us conspire
to efface the exquisite engravings.
It is in the air that the stains on your skirt
have raised eyebrows in the neighbourhood,
and they spit on your footsteps.

But I see every day,
tattoos engraved on tender skin,
with needles of poisonous ink.
I'm alone, and I die lonelier
in this battle against taboos
while friends pretend to follow me to my grave.

Your love for me,
with unspeakable tales of tattoos
inscribed on your thighs
and your screams of apprehension
silenced by the drilling,
make me shout meaninglessly to a small sailing cloud,
which almost hits the moon.

But I gather my weapons,
ready to fight the ugly masks
which cringed your fair, downy skin.
I will cut a reed, burn holes on it,
and blow music to lure away your tattoos
until you fall asleep on green grass.

When it is all over,
I'll bow and accept the end of a love or a reason.
Then I'll pick up a spade and write this poem
on fresh earth under these pines
and lay my head on a log that shifts with a jolt
when I finally whisper your name to a blade of grass.

The Second Best

My love was naked, and she didn't hide.
My heart flew away chasing a raven, her clothes, and
my body covered her nakedness.
When she moved, everything moved—our bodies,
earth, and blood.

Angst of a shadow for not being a tree, and her
dream being the second best, the sadness she caged.
But amidst rustlings of bodies, sweat, panting hearts, and jealous
lovers,
I asked the shadow to shelter courage.
The second best I could do.

Her waist rose up from the pelvis,
a geometry of creation, and my heart came back
with a black feather: a memoir of a flight.
She looked at me, her eyes wrote a dream, and
I published it with puce-coloured covers—a shadowy book.

We've seen dead songs moving with strokes of grey brush—
living, smiling, laughing, and singing silently.
My love, should we call that symphony the second best?
Don't invite deathwatch beetles in your soul, my love, but
stop the death knell and place sweet dreams under the pillow,
for tomorrow comes along with a rainbow hinged to pillars of hope.

Take heed, your wings will soar high, and on a sky-blue canvas,
you'll be painted a black feather without shadows.

And then, amidst applause of clouds before a drizzle,
I'll come and lay my head on your feathery breasts with a wish
to become the second best, reminding you of the days
when we were shadows wobbling down accursed roads.

Mynshwa

He sat on a tree stump,
morning dew rolled down his bare feet,
winter mist settled on his grey hairs,
his eyes shone like a tiger's,
his toenails grew into the soil beneath dead roots,
he tapped a rhythm with his ginger thumb on his ancient pipe
between long puffs, building a smokescreen of furry tobacco fumes
around him.
His name was Mynshwa.

I walked up to him timidly and asked:
'Are you the tiger who prowled the hills
in dark nights when oak branches become heavier
with sleeping gibbons?'

He raised his face, levelled his eyes with mine,
and thundered: 'My children, the woods and the living
need me, and I guard them from the enemies of darkness.
My name is Mynshwa.'

A girl, not taller than his knees, came out
from behind foliage with a wild flower in her hand and hugged him,
her tender arms around his rugged neck
as if holding a rustic book of history and trying to place the flower
between its pages,
and she whispered to his ears:
'You are my father's father, Mynshwa.'

A rainbow bent across the forest,
its colours spreading a dream above us, and I
saw a speck of green smile on his face, a make-believe spring
on that cold day, while a squirrel hopped up a creeper entwined
around a fig tree,
frightened by a strangely coloured frog, which leaped out
of moist undergrowth, croaking: 'You are Mynshwa the brave.'

Red water streams rolled down the hills to meet river Umtru,
which roared through Nongkhyllem forest, its tall trees
resonating: 'You are Mynshwa the tiger, the guardian of the living . . .
Mynshwa! Mynshwa! Mynshwa!'
while untamed winds were raising a storm.
And hearing the roar of a tigress in the wilderness, Mynshwa
stood up,
walked into the woods, holding the girl's tiny hand, and
a dense cloud floated above him, its lightning separating
the world from Mynshwa, who left me alone, stranded with my
thoughts
in the middle of nowhere called Umtasor.

Mynshwa (Khasi): 'once upon a time'.
Umtru (Khasi): a river in the Ri-Bhoi District of the Khasi hills.
Nongkhyllem (Khasi): a dense rainforest in Ri-Bhoi, a wildlife
sanctuary.
Umtasor (Khasi): a small Khasi village on the edge of Nongkhyllem
forest.

A Woody Dream

Night fell on the forest, and spirits of trees emerged to hunt dreams in the woods, riding fireflies. Crickets were wailing, their shrilly orchestra chased me as I ran into dark gaps between giant oak trees and found my senses animated in the slowly spreading night's sorcery. I began to love the sound of life in the forest, the smell of wild mushrooms in the air. The echoes of a stream somewhere in the woods, leaping and rushing down rugged slopes, had mingled with the crickets' marathon symphony. Stars above the forest were not twinkling—might have gone to bed early! We, the two strangers, a tiger and a leopardess, stirred the moon's silvery ocean, flooding the woods. And we churned out a woody dream. Our furs, though differently textured, tried to warm a love which had gone damp with silent sobs of ferns drenched in last night's vociferous precipitation.

'If you really were my beloved, sing to me the crickets' song in my language and put the words between pomegranate's teeth,' she demanded.

'If you really were my beloved, bring out my dream from my heart and put it on your paws as if it is yours,' I roared back.

'Now, my wandering tiger, knead me and make a new country where there are enough willow branches for homeless fruits. Mould a mother out of me,' she pleaded.

'Your spots have eyes and they exile me in your body. Close them so that I may become your citizen. I will then father your children with clouded furs.'

'Yes, I am ready. Occupy me and prowl through my forest. Oh! My beloved stranger.'

'You are beautiful.'

I whispered and whispered until her furs became a vineyard, and I squeezed the clouds sleeping between the vines to make wine and intoxicate the moon.

And we drank. Our necks caressed each other. I saw her ears moving nervously in the gentle night breeze. She crawled on her belly towards an old oak tree. Her face touched the trunk while her paws clawed on its wrinkled bark. I bit the back of her neck and vanished myself into the eye of a hurricane. Time lost its pace, and we floated in a fathomless vacuum. When we finally sacrificed ourselves to defeat a mad god, I saw the moon smeared with blood from a wound in the sky. And we held each other like entangled kites in a whirlpool of blind winds.

'I am now a leftover of a volcano. I have erupted finally,' she moaned.

'I am the memory of a trumpet. I have blown a song in your flames,' I purred back.

'I am your music now,' she answered.

'Tomorrow I will wield a baton and conduct a choir with mutilated breezes from a cemetery of storms,' I concluded sadly like a dead wind.

I then licked her face. She licked mine. And we parted ways. She walked into the woods, her exhausted tongue combing disarrayed furs. I headed back to my den behind a sleeping hill, following my heart, which had gone ahead of me, rustling through tall grasses, humming a stripy tune.

www.ingramcontent.com/pod-product-compliance
Lightning Source LLC
Chambersburg PA
CBHW022115170526
45157CB00004B/1650